# IMPOSSIBLE YEARS

*Impossible Years* ©2021 by **Janelle Cordero**. Published in the United States by Vegetarian Alcoholic Poetry. Not one part of this work may be reproduced without expressed written consent from the author. For more information, please write V.A. Poetry, 643 South 2nd Street, Milwaukee, WI 53204

In memory of Otto Rainer: grandfather, generous mentor and dear friend

September 1, 1925—March 2, 2021

## I.

9 Milk Carton
10 His Condition
11 Bill's Wife
12 Matrei
13 Bobcat Hunting
14 Young Wife
15 Far from the End
16 Smiling at Himself
17 Working on My Faith
18 Something Others Might Want
19 Future for a Small Town
20 The Mountain
21 Attic of His Mind
22 His Dead Mother
23 His Solitude
24 Alone
25 Something Sharp and Cold

## II.

29 First Grade
30 The Party
31 Somewhere Beyond Age
32 Carries On
33 Making Firewood
34 Cruelties, Blessings
35 The Orchard
36 The Night Was Long and Not Easy
37 Beyond Saving
38 Something Sad
39 Maybe Praying
40 All the Gods Lined Up
41 Butch Cassidy
42 Stroke
43 Elk Season
44 Because the Human Touch is Important
45 A Little Wave
46 Unaware and Unharmed

## III.

49 Work
50 Religion
51 Who is God
52 Power Outage
53 Only My Thoughts
54 Will There Be Anything to Touch
55 Five Inches of Snow
56 January 19, 1949
57 Displaced Persons
58 Shoveling the Walks
59 Not a Door
60 Test Results
61 Red Veins
62 Blind Wish

## IV.

65 All Will Be Buried
66 Weather Girl
67 Coughing
68 Quietly Opening Up
69 Let it Be a Good Day
70 Alive Again
71 Unknowable Mysteries
72 Letter to a Dying Man
73 Get My Boots
74 Beautiful Towns of Childhood
75 After the Storm Ends
76 Bathtub
77 Dark Cavern
78 How Bad Will This Get?
79 What Would Last
80 The Deadbeat
81 That's Something
82 What Will Grow

V.

85 Something Blooming
86 Good Land
87 Outside, the Moon
88 Somewhere Up in the Mountains
89 Tercel
90 Wind Chimes
91 The Widow and Her Children

92 Yard Sales in the Nineties
93 Impossible Years
94 Never Be Filled
95 The Morning After You Died
96 Funeral Parlor
97 Stepping Back
98 Stay Here

I.

Milk Carton

I admit to drinking straight from the mouth of the milk carton when I was young. I didn't see the harm in it, and no one had explicitly told me not to. But I also understood it was not something I could do in front of anyone, nor was it something I could talk about. Later on I took to drinking straight from the bottle of Black Velvet my dad kept in the back of the tallest kitchen cabinet, and the same rules applied. This type of behavior reduced me, turned me into a sneak and a thief. When the bottle was almost gone save an inch, I filled it up halfway with water and left it alone. We found other ways to drink, my friends and I. We found other secrets to keep, secrets that were darker and more disappointing. In this way, we grew up.

His Condition

There's a house down the street with fading green paint, asbestos siding, boards over the windows and a lawn that's more thistle than grass. Sometimes a boy smokes on the concrete steps out front and, I swear to God, the kid looks like he's twelve. He stands with his legs out wide and lets the cigarette hang from a limp arm when he's not taking a drag, like he could care less about the whole thing. Like he could care less about the fire he's not supposed to have. I stare at him sometimes with my arms crossed, worrying about his condition. He scowls at me and flicks the butt into the weeds before going back inside.

Bill's Wife

Things are getting harder and harder for Bill's wife. Bill is an alcoholic, and has been for years. Maybe all of his adult life, who knows. Bill's wife has sent him off to a dozen different places for treatment—he spends weeks at these rehab centers in California and Florida and the like. But after a month of so of being home, the same old shit starts up. And he's a mean drunk, let me tell you. He throws things, like plates and bottles. The whole block can hear what goes on inside Bill's house. Bill's wife calls the cops on him once or twice a month, and we all watch from our windows when the cruisers pull up. How long can this kind of unhappiness go on?

Matrei

My great grandparents were born in the Austrian village of Matrei. The town sits in a valley and is surrounded by mountains with white peaks. They left this village for an American town some 8,000 miles away from where they began. This town was also surrounded by mountains, and it was the largest producer of magnesite in the world during the early 20th century. The tallest building was the church thanks to its golden-spired steeple, which was fine by my Catholic grandparents. They didn't plan to stay in America—rather, they just wanted to make enough money to save up for a comfortable lifestyle back in Austria. But they lived here the rest of their lives, in a town named after the water snake where the fields go on forever and the river never runs dry. If I ask questions of them, will they answer me? Tell me, were you happy here? Did you ever look out the window and wish you were someplace else? What did the mountains mean to you, both the ones here and those back home? I keep going with the questions but never get a response, at least not one I can recognize. None of this gets talked about.

Bobcat Hunting

Carver chose writing a poem over going bobcat hunting with his friend Morris. But he ended up writing a poem about bobcat hunting—he wrote about the hounds and the rifle. So, in a sense, he did go hunting. He sat at his desk at six in the morning and the whole scene was right in front of him: Morris and the hounds and the bobcat somewhere nearby, but hidden, like a stand-in for God. Carver didn't believe in God but he believed in stories. Aren't they the same thing?

Young Wife

He wakes up with the realization that someday, he and his young wife will rot under the earth. This woman beside him with her auburn hair and quick smile, she'll decay the same as him. He's thought about death before, but not his own death in this way. Not the physical act of it, the loss of form. His wife is asleep and he moves towards her in bed, wraps an arm around her and pulls her close. He'll give her all the happiness he can while they're here together. When she wakes up, he won't mention any of this. Maybe he'll fall back asleep and forget these thoughts, forget any of this happened.

Far from the End

My grandma grew up in a two-story house along the Colville River. Her mother was a schoolteacher and her father owned the general store. My grandma was an only child, but she had a dog for company. She and the dog would sit on the bank of the river to watch the fishermen struggle with walleye and brown trout. My grandma was very good at staying quiet, so the fishermen liked having her there and would sometimes bring treats for her. A piece of hard candy, a plum, things like that. My grandma loved water all her life. Some forty years later, my grandpa would build her a house alongside Mill Creek with wall-to-wall windows for looking out. They lived in the house almost forty years before she died. But back then, on the river bank with the dog, she was untouched by the future. Far from the great love and the great suffering. Far from the end. She would sit on that bank for hours until someone, usually her mother, called her name.

Smiling at Himself

He didn't brush his teeth until he was 15 or 16 years old. His parents couldn't afford to buy toothbrushes for the six boys, but they couldn't afford candy, either. So their teeth weren't all that bad. But he liked brushing his teeth as a teenager—he liked the routine of it. The luxury. He remembers the powder, how he poured a bit in his palm and then dipped the bristles of the brush in the powder. It would foam in his mouth as he worked the brush around. He remembers spitting the foam out in the sink and smiling at himself in the mirror with his clean teeth. He still does this today, lifetimes later. Spit, smile. It's like Murakami says—no matter how far we go, we can never be anything but ourselves.

Working on My Faith

I'm working on my faith. More specifically, I'm trying to decide what or who to have faith in. The Zen master says great faith and great doubt are inseparable, so I plant them in clay pots and water them side-by-side. I set my faith and my doubt on the back porch where they'll get the best southern sun, and I bring them both inside at night to protect them from spring frost. They turn from seedlings to sprouts to small plants with skinny stalks as I keep up with the routine. I read to them from the Bible and the Buddha's teachings. I tell them about Plath and Sexton. I tell them about current events and play Rachmaninoff for them. I give my faith and my doubt all the evidence I have of human nature— I want them to know everything. And they grow equally as strong and as tall. Soon I have to plant them in the backyard, where they take root and grow skyward. I sit between them in the summer and stare at them from a window in the winter. The Buddha's last words were, practice diligently. Christ's last words were, why have you abandoned me?

Something Others Might Want

A clear afternoon in October, around 55 degrees with no wind or clouds, and he decides to walk the three blocks to the pizza joint on Bridgeport for a warm meal he can bring home. He walks everywhere anyway—no car. Suspended license. But usually he has to walk, no choice about it. This time he decides to walk, because he could have the pizza delivered, or he could just heat up one of the TV dinners from the freezer. The lasagna ones aren't half bad. He has other options is what I'm saying. But you could say he wants to walk this time. He likes the way the sun warms his face while his hands become colder and colder. He likes the way the fallen leaves cover most of the garbage on the sidewalk. When he gets to the pizza place he orders an extra-large cheese, keeps it simple so he won't have to wait long. They hand him a grease-stained cardboard box in no time, and he's out the door again. Steam rises from the corners of the box as he walks home. He's proud to be carrying something warm and fragrant, something others might want.

Future for a Small Town

We hold tight to our styrofoam cups filled with coffee. We bring the cups to our puckered lips and sip delicately not to burn our tongues. Outside the wind rips through the old town. We spend mornings in this diner saying do you remember this or that? We talk of Sherman, who shot his wife and then himself back in the sixties. We talk of Melville, who was a hell of a concrete finisher but also had a drinking problem. The future for a small town like this is something we can't make sense of, but the past we can hold up for measure. We can build things from these memories, like pity and longing. We can understand that everything that's happened in the world has happened here, too. In other words, we haven't missed a thing.

The Mountain

I remember when the mountain caught fire some years ago—our mountain. The mountain named after the town with the white cross near the peak. We all gathered in the grocery store parking lot to watch it burn, torn between fear and something else, something like awe or reverence. The sky was dark with smoke and the air tasted of ash. Some people got down on their knees to pray. It was summer and the asphalt must've been scalding, but there they were, on their knees. Some of them in shorts, no less. The praying scared me more than the fire. The fire was put out before any damage was done to the town. But the mountain stayed charred and black for years until the new trees we planted took hold. Who saved us, and why?

Attic of His Mind

The nuns were old and plain. They moved like shadows through the halls, silent except for the rustling of their black robes. The children were afraid of those nuns, afraid of their pale floating faces. The children sat straight at their desks as the nuns lectured on music or mathematics. When the nuns turned to write on the blackboard, the children made faces at one another. If a child was caught sleeping or daydreaming, the nuns would thwack the child's knuckles with a yard stick. Sometimes the children would whisper theories about what was under those black robes: the body of an insect? Wings? The nuns were another mystery, like God. The nuns are all dead now. My grandfather was one of those children, and he's in his nineties. He keeps them alive in the attic of his mind.

His Dead Mother

His mother has been dead for something like sixty years. Sometimes he returns to childhood in his dreams and he's happy to see his mother in those dreams. She's always doing something useful, like hauling a bucket to the neighbor's house to buy milk from their dairy cow or making soup from bones the butcher saved for dogs. He grew up in the Great Depression, and his mother was an immigrant from Austria. There are so many things I'd like to ask her now, he says, but it's too late. What kinds of things, I say. The little things, he says. I want to know what the name was of the ship she rode to America, or if she had any friends on the ship. I want to know if she had American money in her pockets on the trip over, and how she knew what the coins meant. I'd ask her how she met my father and why they decided to get married. I wish I knew more about her life, he says. Then he stays quiet a while. Maybe you'll still get a chance to ask her all these things, I say, implying something about heaven. This man, who has been Catholic all his life, shrugs his shoulders and smiles. How little we know of death, he says. Now we stay quiet a long time together.

His Solitude

He hasn't left the house in months, but he still gets dressed in the morning, still laces up his Redwings, even. I don't ask him how long it takes to get dressed, to button all the buttons on his khaki shirt. I'm afraid of what the answer will be. Fifteen minutes? Half an hour? What is time when we have too much of it? He gets dressed to go from his bedroom to the living room, where he reads in his leather chair all day. Sometimes he puts his book down to watch birds outside the window. Sometimes he shuts his eyes for a while. His solitude is a sad music, but it's music all the same.

Alone

My mother would only play the piano if everyone else in the house had gone to bed. I remember being in the dark with the quilt pulled up to my chin and the piano notes reaching me from somewhere far off. The music felt very much like a dream. Sometimes I'd have questions about what she was playing, but I didn't dare get out of bed or open my door for fear she'd stop playing altogether. Already, I knew what it meant to be alone, knew how sacred it was.

Something Sharp and Cold

I can't fish anymore. It was hard enough as a kid—I wasn't squeamish about the worm. The hook was the problem, the hook with its cruel pronged point. I remember sitting on the dock with my brother and praying for the fish to leave. Please God, I'd say to myself, don't let a fish bite my line. Imagine how my faith shriveled every time my bobber went under. The worst was when a fish swallowed the hook with the worm. I had to hold the squirming trout with one hand and reach into its mouth with the other. There was always blood. If I couldn't get the hook undone, we had to cut the line. But most of the time I could get the hook undone. Sometimes we kept the trout for our father to grill, and other times we would toss the shocked bodies back into the black water and watch them sink. Swim, I'd pray. Swim, swim away. That was then. I can't fish anymore, not with what I know about pain. I picture something sharp and cold hooking me from the inside, pulling me against my will towards some impossible and blinding light, towards mystery, towards death.

**II.**

First Grade

In first grade I wore denim shorts to school every single day, even in the winter. I was trying to prove something. My parents were divorcing, and I wanted to be tough. So I wore my long denim shorts, hand-me-downs from my older brother, and I wore my black Raiders jersey and a backwards baseball cap. It was a costume that lasted a long while, a uniform that meant I wouldn't cry or talk about my feelings. And after a while of not talking about them my feelings went away, like gods without any worshipers.

The Party

The party was ten miles out in the mountains. The boy's parents were out of town, so he spread the news at school. Once it turned dark we all hitched rides with whoever was lucky enough to have a car. We brought whatever alcohol we could steal from our homes or the gas stations, and once we got to his house we put all the booze on the kitchen table. We were proud of ourselves, proud of what we'd accomplished. We got to work on the drinking and our stockpile dwindled. I ended up in the guest bedroom downstairs with a huge plastic bowl to puke in, the kind of bowl our mothers would fill with fruit salad for a barbeque. That's where I spent the night, hugging that bowl as friends came in every once in a while to check on me, to feel my forehead and things like that. They would sit on the edge of the bed and pet my hair the way girls do. And most of all they guarded the door to make sure no boy could come in to find me lying down, hardly conscious. Terrible things happened in those situations, even back then. Especially back then, when we thought nothing mattered more than anything else, when we thought young was the only age to be.

Somewhere Beyond Age

There's a picture of my grandmother when she was young, in her early twenties, maybe. She's lying down on cream-colored carpet and a sun beam shines on her face and shoulders. Her auburn hair pools around her head in fine curls—the picture is in black and white, but I know her hair is auburn, just like mine. Her head is tilted to the left and she's looking somewhere beyond the edges of the photograph. Her face is pale and smooth. She looks like me and not like me. When people are alive we count their birthdays, but when people are dead we count how many years they've been gone. My grandma is somewhere beyond age now, and I have to keep living with her hair, my hair, that just grows and grows like it's trying to reach the ground. Like it's trying to unearth what's been buried.

Carries On

Suffering, we decide, brings us closer to God. Dogs are barking outside as tree branches shift in the wind. Our neighbor across the street sweeps leaves from his walkway into a pile, and then wind disrupts the pile. He gathers as many leaves as he can with his hands and dumps them into the garbage can. The wind carries on. He carries on. The sky darkens and buries the sun.

Making Firewood

They're making firewood. That's the word they use for it, "making," even though it's more of a deconstruction than anything else. The man's job is to cut the trunk of the fallen tamarack into manageable rounds, and the woman's job is to lift the rounds onto the splitter and operate the machine. Most of the rounds split clean, but there are some that get caught on their own splintered flesh. The woman has to kick those rounds off the machine. The sound of the sharp wedge driving through a round is not a snap but like a slow rip—almost like a piece of fabric being torn in two. The man and the woman work until the sun sets behind the pines, then they load the firewood into the bed of their 1980s Ford pickup. They drive home in happy silence, eager to light the stove.

Cruelties, Blessings

The apple tree produced very little fruit. We climbed it as children and hung from the gnarled branches. The few apples the tree did offer up were always hard and small, so we would pick them and throw them at one another. I threw one at the neighbor girl and hit her in the stomach. Her whole body caved in on itself and she fell to the ground. I thought she died. I took off running—I'm not proud of it. But I couldn't face her pain then, the pain I caused. I can barely face it today, to tell you the truth. Where is she now? Did she go on living beyond that moment? What cruelties has she encountered, what blessings?

The Orchard

The orchard is like something out of a painting. We approach it from the highway above, and there are apple and pear trees for miles. The sky is clear and the Columbia River winds behind the land, barely visible. We see five male pheasants among the trees as we drive towards the warehouse. Most of the apples are shipped out for sale, but they keep some in massive crates for local customers to pick through. We fill up cardboard boxes with all the varieties we can think of: Jonagold, Sweet Bee, Honeycrisp, Fuji, McIntosh. 75¢ a pound for all this, we think, shaking our heads and loading more apples into our boxes. We become greedy about it, but who could blame us? The woman weighs our boxes and we pay in cash. A deaf dog sits in the sun outside the warehouse door, and we pet her before loading the boxes into the trunk. We smell the sweetness of the apples all the way home.

The Night Was Long and Not Easy

The night was long and not easy. One of us woke the other one, and we laid there side by side with our eyes open in the dark. After a minute or two we could make out a few objects in our room: the plant near the window, the dresser, the bench given to us by my grandfather. We become part of the world of things again. We turn towards one another. You tell me to match your breath, and you take long inhales and exhales. You tell me to make my breath heavy, to close my eyes. I do what I'm told. I want to leave the night and wake up only when the sun has returned, when the day is warm and free of shadow.

Beyond Saving

Early morning, still dark out. A bell rings somewhere that wakes me up. I look out the window to see an empty street with the wind blowing. On the outside of the sill there's a spider, and the spider is watching a moth struggle in its web. The wings of the moth are free and flapping hard but its legs are held tight. The spider waits a few more seconds and then drags the moth to the corner of the web, out of sight. The moth is beyond saving now, and I didn't have the right to save it in the first place. I turn a light on in the kitchen and drink coffee until daybreak comes, until everything is out in the open.

Something Sad

Something sad has hold of me this morning. I had no part in my dreams last night—it was like I was watching a movie about the inner worlds of other people. I woke up feeling empty and unimportant, even to myself. I take a cup of coffee out to the front porch and stand there in my bathrobe with bare feet, staring at the street and cars and houses. It's early and no one has left for work yet. A man walks past the house, someone I've never seen before. But I can tell by his clothes he's not going to work: sweat pants, a trench coat and combat boots. I watch him walk to the corner house and bang on the door with his fist. The door opens and the man stands there. I'm too far away to hear what's being said, but this will be an exchange like all the rest. The man digs in the deep pockets of his trench coat for some wadded up bills, and a hand reaches out from inside the house with an offering, a plastic bag of powder or pills. The man in sweatpants is walking away from the corner house now, walking back in the direction from which he came. He passes by again with his hands in his pockets, fingering the plastic edges of his happiness. He's walking much faster than before, and he's actually smiling a little. Why should any of this make me feel better? The sun keeps rising and I go on standing here, waiting for what comes next.

Maybe Praying

I am praying for you, even though you don't want to be prayed for. I don't know who or what I am praying to, but I am on my knees with my forehead on the ground. I whisper words to myself, like please and love and help. I don't know what to ask for, exactly, but I want you to move from gray fog to spring morning in your mind. Sometimes you sing about dying when I'm around, even though losing you is my worst fear. It's like you know this but you don't believe it. Or sometimes you believe it, but not all the time. I'm still on my knees but my mind has gone flat. My eyes are closed but tears still seep out, like groundwater from a hole in the earth. I stay like this for a long time, maybe praying and maybe not praying.

All the Gods Lined Up

Gary Snyder says the Bible's Ten Commandments fall short of real moral righteousness. Sure, we're expected not to kill, but what about war? What about the bomb dropped on Hiroshima? He's asking these things. Snyder says the Christian god is a jealous, power-driven figure that worries all the time. Why serve a god like that when there are plenty of other gods waiting patiently to be noticed? Think of it this way: all the gods are lined up shoulder to shoulder on the soccer field waiting to be picked for your team. The Christian god is scowling and kicking at the grass with his cleats, furious about having to stand next to these lesser gods. Obviously Allah and HaShem feel the same way. They roll their eyes at Shiva and Ganesha. Ahura Mazda and Angra Mainyu ignore the others in line and spend their time jostling one another. This line spans from one end of the soccer field to the other. It's hard to choose, right? The answer isn't as obvious as it seems. That's what Snyder is getting at.

Butch Cassidy

I want to see the world without me. I want to walk unnoticed through the lives of those I love to see what harm I've caused, what blessings I've brought on. I want to die and not die, you see, like Butch Cassidy. Some say he survived the gun battle in Bolivia and returned to America to live in the very same city I live in now. He named himself William T. Phillips and spent three decades as a machinist before dying in 1937. He did what we all long to do: escape death. Temporarily, anyway. The Buddhists say my karmic consciousness will live on. The Christians say my soul is everlasting. It's all very hard to explain.

Stroke

He thinks it was a stroke. One second he was standing in the kitchen fixing a sandwich for lunch, and the next thing he knew he was on the floor. Impossible to know if he lost consciousness—he lives alone. Impossible to know if he cried out for anyone—his dead wife, his grown children, his Catholic God. He couldn't stand up—didn't have the strength for it. He crawled on his hands and knees to the telephone on the coffee table in the living room. He called one grown son after another and repeated the same thing: help me. But he couldn't tell if he was getting through to them—he didn't have his hearing aids in at the time. He put down the phone after a while and laid on the carpet. He told himself this was a temporary condition. Maybe he even slept a while, waiting for someone to find him, to say his name and lift him up, to put his world back in order.

Elk Season

He's going to take a few weeks off work in the fall for elk season. It's less about the killing, he says, and more about walking in the woods by himself. Kind of like yoga for men, another guy says. The hunter doesn't respond to that. He's already far away in his mind, tracking something he just wants to get a good look at. He doesn't want to shoot, but he will if the opportunity comes along. If he has to. He spends the rest of the day half here and half somewhere else, following something that doesn't want to be found.

Because the Human Touch is Important

He's not feeling good, he says. His stomach is upset and he's tired, too tired to walk from his chair in the living room to the bathroom. Too tired to eat anything. And he always has a big breakfast, he says. Toast and oatmeal and hard-boiled eggs. But not today, he says, because of his stomach and how tired he is. I get him a bottle of tums from his wife's vanity. She's been dead seven years this Christmas, and the tums are expired. He has trouble with the cap, so I take it off for him and put a few of the tablets in his hand. He chews them slowly, then closes his eyes for a while. I can hear his stomach gurgling from where I'm sitting, and the whole thing worries me. But he says it's just a twenty-four-hour bug and I don't say any different, because I want to believe that, too. When I stand up to leave he stays sitting down, too tired to stand. I touch his knee twice as I say goodbye because the human touch is important. That's what nurses say, anyway. I drive back to town thinking of him but thinking of other things already, also. Thinking of other, less important things.

A Little Wave

On their first date, he took her to a hamburger joint out of town, some fifteen miles out or so. That way they could talk during the drive and get to know each other. He was 21 or 22, and she was 17. He'd just got back from WWII a few months ago, and he spotted her at a grange hall dance. There were all kinds of dances back then—every weekend you could count on having a dance. He was a good dancer, and she was, too, though not as good as him. When they made it to the restaurant, they each had a hamburger and shared a milkshake. This began a love that lasted sixty years and beyond. She's dead now, and he's lived for seven years without her. But she's still everywhere: in the flower garden she tended, in her book of daily Catholic devotions that sits on her nightstand, in the decorative towels hanging in the guest bathroom, in the toiletries that crowd her vanity. She was more than these things, but they are like extensions of her—kind of like how rivers are extensions of their source. He drives by her grave every day on his way to town. Sometimes he stops, and other times he just gives a little wave and keeps going.

Unaware and Unharmed

We try to compare one death to another. He was hit by a logging truck, we say, so it was instantaneous. He could've been afraid for a second, maybe less. But then it was all over. She died of cancer, so that's worse. We think so, anyway. She had time to get her things in order, sure, but what about all those sleepless nights with her eyes open in the dark? He just drove, unaware and unharmed, towards death. He was getting off work, so he probably had the radio on and the sun would be setting behind those mountains. He was probably happy, right before.

**III.**

Work

I want to spend the morning in silence. I want to read books by my spiritual teachers, and I want to meditate on each passage. I want to write my own words based on their words, and I want my own words to surprise and satisfy me. These are the things I think about as I get out of bed. But then I see the snow outside—inches of it and still falling. How can I sit quietly at my desk when there's work to be done already? How can I ignore the scraping of my neighbor's shovel? I put on my coat, boots, gloves and hat. I step out into the cold, into the movement of the day. I take the shovel from the porch and begin clearing what will be covered again in a few hours. Snowflakes gather on my shoulders and in my hair as I work. I try to keep my mind blank and open. Words are no use out here.

Religion

Andre Malraux writes of the corpse and what it means to believers and nonbelievers. Either way, we are fearful of death. The newspaper says Christianity will become extinct in Britain in less than two decades. Christianity is an animal threatened by those who are "spiritual but not religious." I've said these words once or twice. I can believe some of scripture but not all of it, and therein lies the problem. The religion of my ancestors will die in my hands and in the hands of those like me.

Who is God

The boy is kicking the snowman. White flecks of the body spray everywhere. The boy is seven or eight years old. His mom watches from the front porch. Jack, she says, stop kicking the snowman. Jack doesn't stop. It's my snowman, he says. I built him, and I can destroy him. Bigger chunks of the snowman are falling off now. The mom doesn't respond, just keeps watching the boy. Why does this remind me of God? And who is God: Jack, his mom, or the snowman?

Power Outage

The power was out for forty-eight hours, and the temperatures were well below freezing with two feet of snow outside. He had to keep the wood stove burning the whole time so the pipes wouldn't freeze. The bedroom is the farthest room from the wood stove, and it got down to 41 degrees in there at night. So he slept in the recliner and woke up every 2 hours or so to feed the fire. He didn't eat much during this time—cooking was out of the question. So he had some pie and a few hard-boiled eggs. He brought the dog inside for company, and she slept on the carpet next to the fire. He felt far from everything. The power came back on right before he ran out of wood, right before things took a turn for the worst. It took him a few nights to get used to sleeping in the bed again, to stop waking up in the middle of the night and looking for that orange glow.

Only My Thoughts

I've spent hours by myself in this little room. I've chosen solitude over anything else, and I wonder if this was the correct decision. The moral one, even. Maybe what is more virtuous and more difficult would be better. Maybe instead of spending so much time in this room, I need to be out there caring for all the sick. Those who are struggling. Tell me, am I selfish? For wanting only my thoughts today and nothing else?

Will There Be Anything to Touch

White snow on the branches of black trees. Here's what I'm beginning to understand—the next world will be nothing like this one. Here there are mountains, rivers, endless highways. Here there are buildings and windows and alleyways and even homes with front porch swings and vegetable gardens. Here I have a body with hips and freckles and hands, most of all, hands. Will there be anything to touch in the world beyond this one? Will there be anything to pick up and hold against me, the way children do with their toys?

Five Inches of Snow

Five inches of snow fell in the afternoon, and in my mind I was a child again. I was back in the town of 5,000 where us kids would walk to the sledding hill with our plastic toboggans dragging behind us. When we got to the top of the hill we would take a running leap onto our sleds and sail full-speed towards the bottom. Sometimes we would build jumps for our sleds if the snow was the right consistency. The walk from the bottom of the hill to the top took a few minutes, so we would take a break halfway up to sit down and eat snow. This was how we spent those winter days. Once it got dark, we would walk home for hot chocolate. I remember the warm glow of the street lamps and the swishing noises our snow pants made. Sometimes we would go back out after the hot chocolate for night sledding. I can see the soft flakes falling and gathering on our knit caps, our shoulders. We would squint from the top of the hill down towards the bottom to try and make out the path clearly. Think of it now: the night sky overhead and the town lights in the distance. Nothing compares.

January 19, 1949

They were the first couple to get married in the new Catholic Church on 3rd. She was 18 and he was 23. She wore a long-sleeved lace dress and styled her auburn hair in curls. He wore a black suit. Both sets of parents were there, along with all five of the groom's brothers. The bride was an only child. I've seen pictures of them right after the ceremony—they're standing on the church steps outside. The white snow, the white church, and his black suit. Their big smiles and white teeth.

Displaced Persons

He and a few soldiers stayed behind in Europe after the victory over Germany. There was a lot of work to do, he said. A lot of clean up. Millions of people were displaced from the war, he said, and they wandered like nomads. Some had survived the concentration camps, while others had survived the bombings of towns and major thoroughfares. Most had no home or family to return to, so they walked from place to place with their impossibly skinny bodies and their heavy grief. The U.S. soldiers always ate good, he said, and there were a lot of times when we couldn't finish what was on our plates. We would scrape the food into a garbage pail, he said, and later the displaced persons would root through the trash with their thin fingers. I took to leaving my plate with food on it next to the garbage can, he said. I would purposefully take more than I could eat so there would be some left over. They never looked up when they arrived, just stared down at whatever food they could find. They hardly made a sound. We believed they could get better over time, he said. We believed we could all be healed.

Shoveling the Walks

The whole block is out before sunrise shoveling the walks. Well, most of the block, except the couple with all the kids. And I guess the alcoholic with the Canadian accent isn't out here, either. But most everybody else is scraping at the concrete with their shovels, digging out their cars and the like. We all wave to one another but there's no talking—we have work to do. We start to sweat under our winter jackets, because the snow is wet and heavy. Some of us take off our gloves, even, and our hands turn red from the cold. But we keep at it. We slowly unearth what's ours. And the sun, it does the same.

Not a Door

Death is not a door—we can't describe it the way we try to describe everything else. Objects can't help us here, and neither can comparisons. Death is death—that's the closest we'll get. The social scientist says the majority of people who say they believe in God don't really believe in God, because their lives don't reflect the morals of their religion. In other words, if they actually believed in God they would try harder to be better people. The scientist said we don't really believe we're going to die. Is death our greatest incentive for believing in something beyond what we have here? The Buddhist abbot says all attachments are based in fear. We are conscious now—can't that be enough?

Test Results

He's waiting on the test results for his cancer. He pictures an oil spill spreading through his innards, the black sludge seeping into every organ one-by-one. He spends his days in a junkyard dismantling old Volkswagens, taking parts from one to build up another. Most of the car bodies are rusted through, scattered among the overgrown grass like metal carcasses. The whole place is a reminder of death. He's a carpenter by trade, but he can't face working with wood right now. He can't handle the fresh-cut boards, some of them still bleeding sap from the grain. He doesn't want to build anything while knowing it will all be undone. So he spends his days alone in this junkyard waiting for the young doctor to call, waiting for news on his condition and hoping all will be revealed soon.

Red Veins

There was a time when I didn't smile or laugh as a child. The adults in my family were suffering through these arguments, these yelling matches and weeping contests. So I wanted to be tough, see. If I started crying there would be no stop to it, and it was the same with laughing. So I kept my face still as stone, and my blue eyes whirled around, taking in the sadness and the sunlight after. I was beginning to understand silence and its power. After a while the adults would stop yelling and turn to me, wondering about my condition. They would grab hold of my shoulders and bring their faces inches from mine. I remember the red veins snaking through the whites of their eyes. I would follow those veins as they stared at me, trying to decide what all this means.

Blind Wish

The surface of the creek is covered with ice and snow, but the water still flows like a vein under the skin. Trout settle in deep pools at the bottom of the creek where the water is more stable. They gather in groups to ride out the winter, moving as little as possible and eating drifting insects. Many trout die of starvation if the winter is long and cruel. I think of their gleaming speckled bodies in the darkness, their patience and their blind wish for spring.

**IV.**

All Will Be Buried

The radio is all politics this morning, so I switch it off and drive in silence. This gives me time to think, to pay attention. I see five dead deer alongside the highway and one dead cat. I make note of everything, but I understand very little. The road takes me deeper into the mountains. Snow begins to fall—the heavy flakes that build up fast. There's a sense that all will be buried in this snow: the mountains, the road, my car, the dead animals. Everything will be covered equally and completely, and none of this will matter. But I keep driving anyway, squinting through the windshield and making my tracks through the mystery, through the white stillness.

Weather Girl

In high school my plan was to be a weather girl. I was pretty enough for it, or at least my friends said so. Weather girls seemed polished and glamorous on television, and they all spoke with such confidence about this storm or that stretch of sunshine. Maybe wanting to be a weather girl was less about the weather and more about wanting to know something, anything. Wanting to look up at the sky and understand.

Coughing

He's out on his porch coughing something terrible. I mean it—sounds like he's trying to cough his soul out of his body. He has a cigarette in one hand and he uses the other hand to cover his mouth while he coughs. He works construction so he's out of the house by seven, but he always stops for a smoke on the porch before starting his truck and driving towards the jobsite. He'd give up smoking if he could, but it's like meditation for him. The only time his mind is quiet is when there's a cigarette in his hand. He stops coughing and flicks the butt into the snow-covered lawn. The rain will wash away the snow soon enough, and everything will be exposed. He starts his truck and pats the front pocket of his coat, checking that his soul is still intact, maybe, or feeling for the pack of Marlboros he keeps there.

Quietly Opening Up

Smoke from the chimney hangs low in the cold clean sky. It's almost Valentine's Day, almost time to start seedlings in the greenhouse, almost time to rake the matted grass and clear away the branches that fell from the boxwood with every heavy snowfall. There are always things to look forward to, but what can I love about this morning in between? What can I love about scraping ice from the windshield? What can I love about the long drive north? The day is quietly opening up, and I'm at the center of everything.

Let It Be a Good Day

Let it be a good day. Let work go by fast. Let it be a day without personal or global disaster. Let there be good news on the radio for the drive to work. Let the sun come out. Let my words match my intentions. Let no harm be done to me, and let me honor everyone I come in contact with. Let my prayers be answered. Let me know someone or something is listening.

Alive Again

At his age he's learned love takes on many different shapes and forms, like a cloud being pushed around by the wind. Love is the cloud and everything else is the wind. This new gal has moved in with her little dog and the house is full of noise all the time. Good noise, like humming and the clanking of dishes and her footsteps coming towards him down the hallway. He's lived alone for years and the house feels alive again. Best yet is the little dog, how she sits with him in the chair in the evenings and goes to sleep, warm and content. Sometimes he puts his hand on the dog's side to feel breath moving through its body, rising and falling, and then he takes a nap, too. His girlfriend will find them this way sometimes, the dog and him with their eyes closed, dead to the world as the unwatched cable news lists one disaster after another. What could be better? She lets them sleep.

Unknowable Mysteries

As a child I was afraid of ghosts. Ghosts, death, all the unknowable mysteries. As an adult, I am afraid of loss. Loss is just another word for ghosts, for death, but it's less shameful to say. The other adults understand this—we talk of loss in broad daylight. So and so lost his job, the neighbor lost her husband, someone's cousin lost his ranch to the bank. Perhaps the idea of loss is more childish than ghosts—if something is lost, there's still hope of finding it someday. Each death is a loss. Each death is a ghost pulling at our bedsheets at night, whispering our name.

Letter to a Dying Man

I'm writing a letter to a dying man, and I want to write please don't die, because I don't understand the world without you. But I realize this would be a selfish thing to say, so instead I write, I miss you. I hope you are not in pain. Remember to say the rosary. I'm not Catholic, but he is, and the rosary gives him comfort. I stop myself from asking, are you afraid of death? Or, do you believe in ghosts? I ask, do you remember the nuns from your childhood? Do you remember the white church with the copper steeple? I picture him reading this letter and nodding yes, yes. His mind will go back to those days of childhood spent in that small town of wheat fields and distant mountains where he and his brothers slept three to a bed and his immigrant parents learned English by reading the dictionary. And maybe for a moment he will forget about his collapsing lungs and failing heart, he'll forget about the hospital room with its fluorescent lights and beige walls and nurses like astronauts in PPE gear. He'll close his eyes and be a young boy again, walking to school with books under his arm and a whole life of mystery ahead of him.

Get My Boots

I asked the nurse if he was dying. She shrugged and said we're all dying. She couldn't help me, I decided. She probably couldn't help him, either. So I kept my mouth shut around the nurses after that. I watched as they strung tubes and wires from the machine inside his body to the machines outside of his body. They wiped his nose and eyes and forehead with a damp washcloth. They put more pillows behind his head and draped wool blankets on top of him, one after another. None of this will save him. Where are my boots, he asked me one day. I need to get dressed, he said. I need to get the hell out of here. This from a man who can't get out of bed by himself, who can't stand up without a nurse on either side of him. This from a man who spent most of his life building house after house in this small town, buying plats of land and building whole neighborhoods. This from a man who could lug a full five-gallon bucket of paint up a two-story ladder well into his eighties. This from a man who lay in bed beside his wife of sixty years and held her hand as she moved from this world to another. Get my boots, he said again. So I reached for boots that weren't there. I believed, just for a moment, in what couldn't be, in what will never be again.

Beautiful Towns of Childhood

The beautiful towns of childhood wait for us to return. The playgrounds in the park are still gleaming and dangerous, and the cashier at the grocery store keeps candy in her pocket for girls and boys who wait quietly in line with their mothers. Lilacs are always in bloom, even in the gauze of winter, and every house looks freshly painted. The teachers are kind and unblemished, and the school textbooks read like fairy tales. The adults in these towns are all tall and well-dressed: the men keep their shirts tucked in, even while mowing the lawn or replacing the alternator in their car, while the women wear shin-length dresses with ironed pleats that refuse to wrinkle. The adults were once the children who played on the swing sets and read the same textbooks—they will spend their entire lives in those beautiful towns. And when they die they'll be buried in the hillside cemetery and remembered with bouquets of flowers every spring. Every childhood town has a river winding around it that tightens every year, like a noose.

After the Storm Ends

We drive north after the storm ends. My husband takes back roads we've never been on before. We don't have any place in mind to go, which is the best strategy for taking a drive. The sun cuts through the clouds as it sets and everything is wet and gleaming; the trees, the tall grasses, the massive houses set back from the road. We drive farther away from the city limits and the houses grow smaller and more desolate. But the sun and the fresh rain from the storm give everything tragic beauty, even the rusting trailers and tarped roofs. We roll down our windows and inhale deeply. We're lost, we decide, but it doesn't matter. We are between everything we know and everything we don't know.

Bathtub

Every night I bury my body in the bathtub. I bury it with water instead of dirt, but it's still good practice. I close my eyes and my thoughts. I stay completely still. I pretend I no longer exist, just to see how the world would do without me. The sounds of living come through from outside: the neighbor's dog barking at a plane overhead, the slam of a car door, someone playing the piano. See, I tell myself, the world exists beyond my conception of it. I keep my eyes closed until the bath water turns cold.

Dark Cavern

He no longer smiles when he sees me. Instead, he stares with his mouth just barely open, like he's unsure of who or what will harm him. He doesn't know what form death will take when it comes, so he has to be suspicious of everyone, even those he loves. I can't blame him. I talk of simple things, like the snowstorm over in Seattle or the bear that used to climb the apple tree on his property. He nods, never takes his eyes off my face. His eyes are bigger than they've ever been as his skin recedes, ready to reveal the bone, the dark cavern of the socket.

How Bad Will This Get?

You ask, how bad will this get? This is the worst part, your daughter says. She's talking about death, or rather, she's talking about what comes right before. We keep the blinds in your hospital room closed, because sunlight hurts your eyes. Sometimes you want us to hold your hand, and other times you cry out if we touch your impossibly small shoulders or kiss your forehead. The thin skin of your forearms is stretched tight over the buildup of fluid, and your hands are swollen and smooth. The last thing you eat on this earth is a bowl of canned peaches, the slices cut up into tiny pieces that still take you so long to get down. You nod after each bite and open your mouth, wanting more, waiting for the cold spoon to touch your lips, waiting for more of the sweet gold fruit you've loved all your life.

What Would Last

We spent the afternoon planting flowers. We dug our bare hands into the dark earth to make room for lobelia and alyssum and marigold. It took us ten minutes under the hose water to scrub our hands clean, and we still had dirt under our fingernails for hours after. But the flowers did something for our spirits. We woke the next day to a storm of violent proportions and watched from the window as our flowers were pushed around by the wind and beaten with rain. We held each other and wondered what would make it, what would last.

The Deadbeat

She's yelling at him now, calling him a bastard and a deadbeat loud enough for the whole block to hear. They've been married 27 years, but none of us have seen them kiss or even hold hands. He's a drinker, see, and she lost her patience with him long ago. So she yells at him every once in a while, but he never yells back. When she's finished, he walks outside to the front lawn and stares at the sun like he's trying to figure things out. He stands out there for a long time, maybe hoping for someone to walk by and ask how he's doing. Maybe hoping for a plane to fly overhead so he can pretend he's going wherever those passengers are going. Hoping for something, anything, to happen.

That's Something

We don't talk about his cancer. He's waiting on tests, anyway, and knows little about what's going on inside his own body. His hair is longer than I've ever seen it, down past his shoulders, and his beard touches his chest. His jeans are held up by his belt alone. We stand on the shoreline and stare at the snow-capped mountains beyond the lake. Summer is still a long ways off, but the sun is out today. That's something.

What Will Grow

I touch each raspberry stalk and try to decide which ones are dead, which ones are alive. The dead wood feels brittle and hollow, and often the bark will peel. The bark is the skin—is that true? When I find dead stalks I clip them an inch from the ground. Sometimes I clip live stalks on accident, and it hurts to see their green insides. I apologize out loud when this happens. Soon there's a whole pile of dead stalks on the ground. I gather as many as I can and walk them towards the trash—they give me small red cuts on my wrists and forearms. I rub at the cuts for hours afterwards, thinking of the dead bark, thinking of skin and how it must peel away from our bodies once we're buried. Does this happen? What will grow from the death of me? What will shoot from my chest and crawl its way through the dirt towards the sun, towards what is green?

V.

Something Blooming

The air is sweet this morning. The streets are still wet from last night's rain, but the sky is clear now. I stand on the porch a long time, inhaling deeply. I close my eyes and listen to my own breath instead of the sounds of traffic on the nearby arterial. It's easy to believe more in spirit and less in body during these moments. I become a ghost—I disappear into the smell of something blooming.

Good Land

The dirt just below the surface is dark and teeming with life. We pick the dirt up by the handful and crumble it between our fingers. This is good land, we tell each other. We feel rich standing on it. We don't have to survive off the land, not yet. Not like my great grandfather did, a farmer with acres and acres near the river. Those fields of his were filled with gold—that's how it felt during the Great Depression, anyway. He wasn't a wealthy man, but his family always had food on the table. The food was the gold, see. The milk, the vegetables, the eggs, the meat. His two boys, one of them my maternal grandfather, grew to be six feet tall. All because of those fields with their rich dirt, like this dirt here. This dirt in my hands almost a century later, hundreds of miles away.

Outside, the Moon

We take a drive around the city and point things out to one another like children do. Dog, I say. Flower, he says. Cop, I say. River, he says. After each thing is named we nod and smile with appreciation. We build the city one noun at a time. Fountain, I say. Cathedral, he says. Graveyard, I say. Deer, he says. Hours pass and the street lamps switch on one by one. Moon, I say. Moon, he says. We have no need to name anything in the dark. We drive home, silent and happy with our work. Our bed is cold, so we wedge ourselves together. Love, I say. Love, he says. Outside, the moon.

Somewhere Up in the Mountains

He's the type to take a long drive just for the hell of it. He likes the mountains up north best for their snaking roads, the river and the fields of wildflowers. He could keep driving forever, through Canada and into Alaska. He'd even drive into the ocean, if he could. But somewhere up in the mountains he remembers me, says my name out loud, maybe, and turns around to come home.

Tercel

The dirt road was rutted from runoff, with woods on either side of cedar, pine and tamarack. Always blue skies above, because there's no other way to imagine those summer days when we'd take the Toyota Tercel for a long drive through the backcountry. My brother and I were young at the time, maybe six and eight. Dad would lift us one at a time onto his lap and tell us to steer. We were thrilled but also sobered by the responsibility. We took steering very seriously. We stared straight-faced through the windshield and kept our small hands on the wheel, forgetting all about our dad and the brake under his foot, believing we were in control.

Wind Chimes

I woke late at night to the sound of wind chimes and thought it was music. I got out of bed and walked from one room to the next, listening for the source of the sound. The mystery of it made me uneasy. I went back to bed without an answer, the far off music still playing somewhere. When I opened my eyes in the morning I heard the chimes again, and I knew what the sound was right away. Music, yes, but the kind we can't sing along to, or memorize. Music made for this moment, and no other.

The Widow and Her Children

The widow and her children are at the park on Mother's Day. The children are all adults, tall daughters, lovely in their flowing skirts. The father died a few months back, around the same time the snow began to melt. So the mother is newly widowed, and her sadness is a heavy shroud atop her black dress. The widow and her children walk along the riverbank and pick the wildflowers. The widow picks a flower, brings it to her face as she inhales deeply, then tosses it into the water. She watches the flower flow downriver until she can no longer see the flash of color bobbing in the current far off, and then she picks a new flower. She does this over and over again, a practice in letting go. Her children leave the park with their fists full of wildflowers, but the mother's hands are empty. Maybe for the first time in her life.

Yard Sales in the Nineties

Every Saturday in the summertime I went to yard sales with my mother and grandmother. I'd have ten bucks in my pocket, maybe, and a few quarters. There was a whole curio shelf in my room dedicated to yard sale finds: oriental fans with delicate paintings of rivers and mountains, seashells, tiny wooden clogs, books in different languages. I don't remember the kinds of things my mother or grandmother would buy, though my grandmother collected teddy bears. Their purchases were probably more practical, like dishware or furniture or floor rugs. I always finished looking over a yard sale before they did, so I'd go sit on some curb and wait. I didn't mind the waiting. I watched people pick things up and put them down, the air heavy with consideration. Women would hold blouses to their chests and purse their lips. Men took swings with the used golf clubs up for sale, while children dug through cardboard boxes overflowing with stuffed dolls and plastic dinosaurs. Yard sales were treasure hunts back then—no one felt ashamed about rummaging through the belongings of their neighbors. You'd see the richest lady in town next to the poorest lady in town, both of them fussing over the same decorative plate for a quarter. When it was time to go, the three of us would climb back into mom's minivan to check the next listing in the newspaper. Once we hit all the sales, it was time for ice cream back at the house. I'd get everything I wanted on those Saturdays, even if I didn't buy anything.

Impossible Years

Nearly everything is forgotten, everything but those impossible years of childhood. There were always woods nearby, woods of pine and fir and cedar with dirt paths like fairy tales. Ferns and clover and fallen pinecones, the sunlight shifting through the trees. It was easy to believe in everything back then: God, magic, good and evil, heaven. Heaven, most of all. Nothing made sense without heaven. We didn't know the woods were heaven. We didn't know childhood was heaven, the eternity of those years. Now we know. We are so far away from those times, from those woods with the dirt trails and roots splitting the ground.

Never Be Filled

Bukowski says there's a place in the heart that will never be filled, and I know just what he's talking about. He doesn't define it, but I will: the space of awareness, the space of time and change and death. The space of emptiness, truly. The space that will endure long after we're gone.

The Morning After You Died

The morning after you died was bright and cold. The moon and the sun hung on opposite ends of the gray-blue sky and I didn't know what God to pray to for comfort. I thought of the way your hands worked the rosary like a familiar tool as you spoke softly of the great mysteries. You told me once that you were jealous of those who could hear the voice of God, plain and unadorned. You died with the rosary resting on your chest. You died in a dark room among the whirs and beeps of medical equipment. You died wearing a green hospital gown instead of the khakis you wore to work for decades. You died—that's what I'm trying to say. I still don't believe it.

Funeral Parlor

The body in the casket is too thin, and the lips are the wrong color. Too dark. Someone nearby says well, he doesn't exist anymore. I open my mouth to argue but don't know where to start. So I turn away from the body. I close my eyes and whisper to the one we've lost. Tell me where you are now, I say. Tell me where we're all going to end up. I move from the dark room to the lobby of the funeral parlor. Afternoon sun spills onto the cream carpet, the floral wallpaper. The funeral director stands tall and handsome in the corner, pale hands clasped in front of him. He bows his head at my grief and I see his widow's peak, time working away at his youth, death coming for us all in its own slow way. I smile, nod and step out into the sun, the world of the living.

Stepping Back

I sat closest to your casket at the funeral. When the priest swung the censer above the white pall sheet, I could smell frankincense and myrrh. I learned afterwards the smoke from the incense is meant to symbolize our prayers for the dead rising towards heaven. The procession to the cemetery drove by an elementary school, and some of the children stopped playing tetherball or tag to stare at the hearse. The gravesite was a perfect rectangle, dark and deep beneath the blue sky. Songbirds called to one another from the pine trees as the priest sprinkled holy water over the casket before stepping back, crossing himself and closing his eyes.

Stay Here

The alarm goes off and I reach for it. You reach for me and say stay, stay here. We can stay here forever, you say. I close my eyes and settle into you. We both know something will wake us: the birds outside, the bells of the high school next door, our own hunger. But for now the house is dark and no one needs us. We sleep but don't dream.

Acknowledgements

"Something Others Might Want" first published in *SLANT*

"Milk Carton" first published in *Steam Ticket*

"Weather Girl" and "First Grade" first published in *Sprout Club*

"Something Sharp and Cold" first published in *Cabildo Quarterly*